QUALITY ELECTRIC LAMPS
A PICTORIAL PRICE GUIDE
$ 25.–

Quality Electric Lamps

A Pictorial Price Guide

Edited By L-W Book Sales

2nd Printing 1996
L-W Book Sales

Published By:
L-W Book Sales
P.O. Box 69
Gas City, IN 46933

Cover Design: David Devon Dilley
Interior Design: David Devon Dilley

2nd Printing 1996
L-W Book Sales

Published by:
L-W Book Sales
P.O. Box 69
Gas City, IN 46933

ISBN# 0-89538-009-9

TABLE OF CONTENTS

INTRODUCTION

This book has been put together from many different sources, including: lamp dealers, auctioneers, collectors, etc. The book has been edited by L-W Book Sales and we have tried to make it as best as we can. This book is not meant to be a scholarly work on lamps. It is an illustrated guide with an accompanying price guide. Mistakes have been known to happen with humans and if you do find any (which we are sure you will) we are very sorry, but you must realize that many people contributed to this book and mistakes do happen. There are many different brands of lamps in this book and we could not check authenticity on all of the lamps, so we trusted the contributors on authenticity of the lamps. Sometimes it is hard for even the contributors to identify a lamp correctly. We have tried to include examples of the most important brands and types of lamps. We will have missed some brands of lamps, but if this book is successful we will hope to have a second volume. We hope that this book will help you identify and price the lamps in your collection or lamps that you might be looking for. We also hope you enjoy this book.

Sincerely,
The Editors

The enclosed Price Guide is of current market values. In some regions of the country the prices will vary. You must remember that this is only a guide and meant to be used as such. We are not responsible for any loss or gain of money from selling or buying of the lamps. This is only a Price Guide to assist you in getting a general idea of the prices.

We would like to thank everyone who sent us pictures and information. If we could not use your picture because of quality or other reason we are truly sorry. We also had some problems reading some addresses and names and hope that we came up with the correct information. If we did make a mistake on your lamp information please accept our apology.

Collectors & Contributors / Dealers & Restorers

Cincinnati Art Gallery-635 Main St.-Cincinnati, OH 45202
Garth's Auction Inc.-Box 369-Delaware, OH 43015
David Kurtz-Urbana, IL 61801
McAllister Auction Service-958 Maynard Rd.-Portland, MI 48875
Prater's Auction Service-50600 St.Rt.14 Unity-East Palestine,OH 44413
Kimball Sterling-125 Main St.-Jonesboro, TN 37659
Don Treadway Gallery-2128 Madison Rd.Cincinnati, OH 45208
Chris Olah/Century Antiques-7410 Lorain-Cleveland, OH 44102
Edward Malakoff/Pairpoint Lamp Museum-276 Princeton Dr.- River Edge,N.J. 07661
House of Anteiks-4008 College-Synder, TX 79549
James Roush/Antiques Ltd.-739 W. 5th-Marion, IN 46952

Signed Bradley & Hubbard Piano Lamp - 1900's
McAllister Auction Service
Portland, MI

Bradley & Hubbard - 24" T, 16" Diam. Shade
Prater's Auction
East Palestine, OH

Signed Bradley & Hubbard
Prater's Auction
East Palestine, OH

Bradley & Hubbard
David Kurtz
Urbana, IL

Chicago Mosaic Lamp Co., Signed Leaded Lamp
1910 - 24" Diam. Shade
Chris Olah - Century Antiques
Cleveland, OH

Chicago Mosaic Lamp Co., Signed Leaded Lamp
1915 - 18" Diam. Shade
Chris Olah - Century Antiques
Cleveland, OH

Chicago Mosaic Lamp Co., Leaded Floral
1910 - 18" Diam. Shade
Chris Olah - Century Antiques
Cleveland, OH

Chicago Mosaic Lamp Co., Leaded Floral
1910 - 24" Diam. Shade
Chris Olah - Century Antiques
Cleveland, OH

Panel Lamp - Cincinnati Iron Works
David Kurtz
Urbana, IL

Floral Poppy Classique - 18" Diam.
David Kurtz
Urbana, IL

Birds Classique - 18" Diam.
Private Collector

Classique - 18" Diam.
David Kurtz
Urbana, IL

Signed Classique
David Kurtz
Urbana, IL

Parrot - Consolidated
Prater's Auction
East Palestine, OH

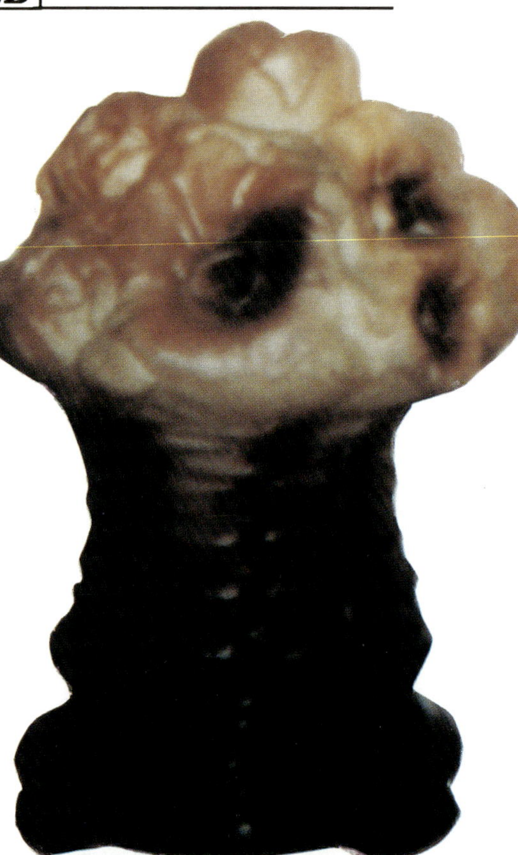

Puffy Flowers - Consolidated
Prater's Auction
East Palestine, OH

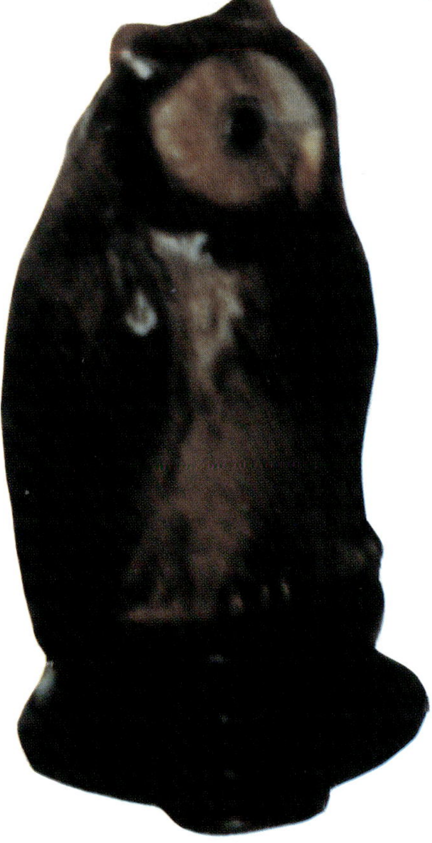

Owl - Consolidated
Prater's Auction
East Palestine, OH

Blown-out Fruit - Consolidated
Prater's Auction
East Palestine, OH

Consolidated
Prater's Auction
East Palestine, OH

Dirk Van Erp - Hammer Copper Table Lamp
Don Treadway Gallery
Cincinnati, OH

Dirk Van Erp - Copper & Mica
Don Treadway Gallery
Cincinnati, OH

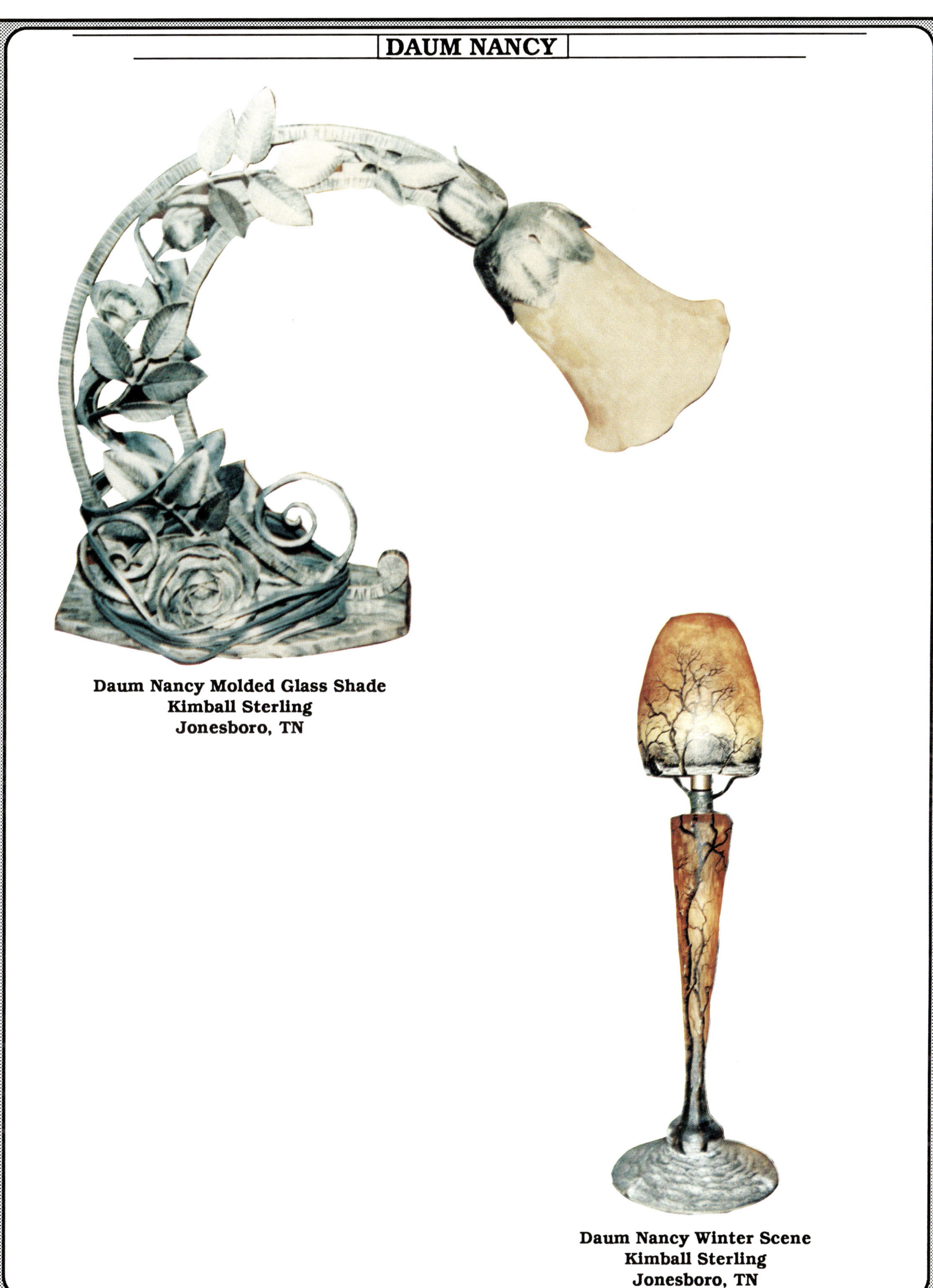

Daum Nancy Molded Glass Shade
Kimball Sterling
Jonesboro, TN

Daum Nancy Winter Scene
Kimball Sterling
Jonesboro, TN

LOUIS XIV

The style of this Period is massive and ornate, but always balanced, and executed with fine dignity, as this royal lamp shows.

ELECTRIC LAMPS

representing all the Periods from the Classic to the Modern are on exhibition at our specially designed show-rooms, Eighth Floor, 11 West 32nd Street, New York. We would call attention to the artistic superiority of these Lamps. Each one possesses decorative individuality that not only gives it value as an æsthetic unit, but that also classes it with some decorative school and so makes it available for use in Period decoration.

ITALIAN RENAISSANCE

Gorgeous and stately, flushed with the colors of grape and sun and sky, this notable work of art stands as a wonderful representation of this Period of the Italian awakening.

THE DUFFNER & KIMBERLY COMPANY
11 WEST 32D STREET NEW YORK

VIKING

The bold and venturesome characteristics of these Sea Rovers are noted in this Electric Lamp, with its shade of rich barbaric colors, adorned with prow-like heads of sea monsters.

ROMAN

The Roman architecture and decoration, with all the imperial desire for imperishable beauty, have all been shown forth in this Electric Lamp.

DKCo

Original Catalog Page

Duffner-Kimberly Leaded Hanging Lamp - 1930's
McAllister Auction Service
Portland, MI

Duffner-Kimberly #189 - 18" Diam.
Private Collector

Duffner-Kimberly - 19 1/2" Diam.
Private Collector

Signed Duffner-Kimberly Leaded
23" Tall - 19" Diam. Shade
Don Treadway Gallery
Cincinnati, OH

Duffner-Kimberly Lamp
Kimball Sterling
Jonesboro, TN

Duffner-Kimberly Lamp
Kimball Sterling
Jonesboro, TN

Duffner-Kimberly Lamp
Kimball Sterling
Jonesboro, TN

Duffner-Kimberly
Kimball Streling
Jonesboro, TN

Duffner-Kimberly - 16" Diam.
Kimball Sterling
Jonesboro, TN

Duffner-Kimberly
Kimball Sterling
Jonesboro, TN

Signed Fulper Lamp - 9 1/2" Tall, 6 1/2" Wide, 19" Long
Prater's Auction
East Palestine, OH

Signed Fulper (top & bottom)
16 1/2" T, 15 1/2" Diam.
Prater's Auction
East Palestine, OH

Green Fulper Perfume Lamp
Prater's Auction
East Palestine, OH

Signed Fulper Figural Nite Lite
Prater's Auction
East Palestine, OH

Gustav Stickley - Brass - 25" L x 6" W
Don Treadway Gallery
Cincinnati, OH

Gustav Stickley Desk Lamp #501 - 16" T
Don Treadway Gallery
Cincinnati, OH

Handel Leaded Lamp - 24" Diam.
Chris Olah - Century Antiques
Cleveland, OH

Handel Poppy Flower
Prater's Auction
East Palestine, OH

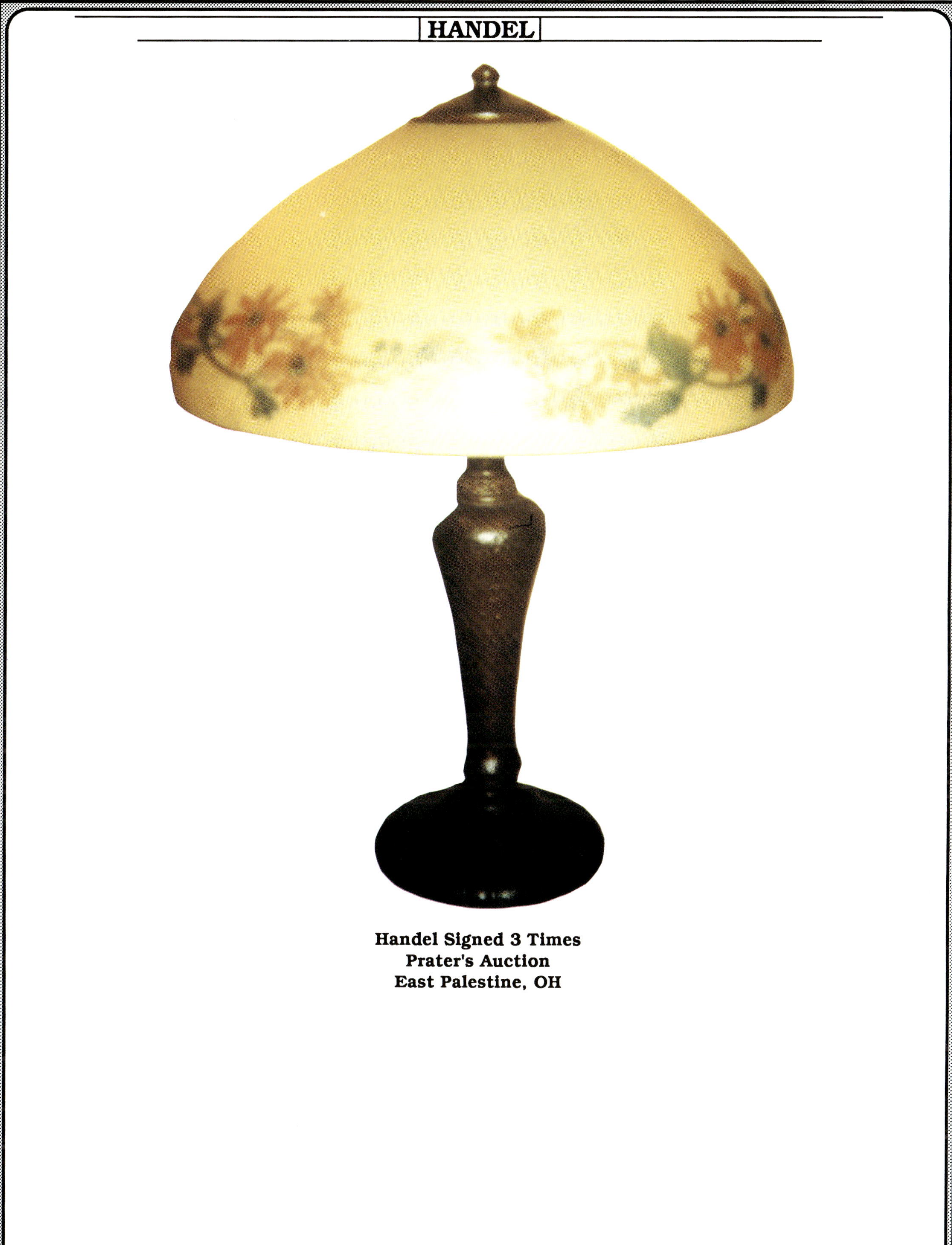

Handel Signed 3 Times
Prater's Auction
East Palestine, OH

Handel - 18" Diam. Shade
Prater's Auction
East Palestine, OH

Handel Scenic Lamp - 18" Diam.
Private Collector

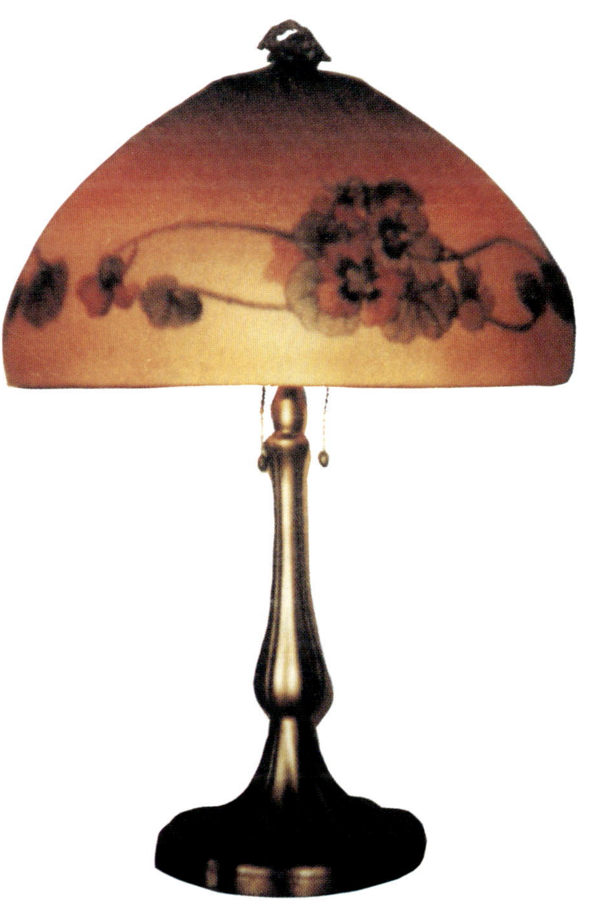

Handel Shade Signed 3 Times - 18" Diam.
Prater's Auction
East Palestine, OH

HANDEL

Handel - 14" Diam. Shade, 20 1/2" T
Prater's Auction
East Palestine, OH

Signed Handel Base with Tiffany Shade
Prater's Auction
East Palestine, OH

Handel Border Lamp
Kimball Sterling
Jonesboro, TN

Handel Deco "Birds"
Private Collector

Handel Boudoir Lamp #6563 - 8" Diam.
Kimball Sterling
Jonesboro, TN

Handel Leaded Lamp
Kimball Sterling
Jonesboro, TN

Handel Peacock
Kimball Sterling
Jonesboro, TN

Handel Lamp
Kimball Sterling
Jonesboro, TN

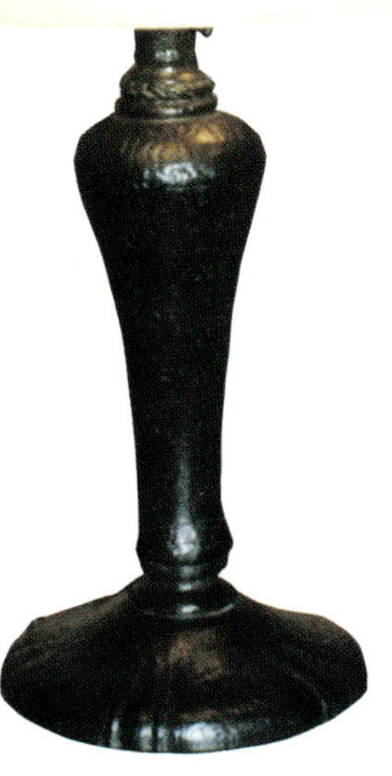

Signed Handel, Blackeye Susan Border - 18" Diam.
Chris Olah - Century Antiques
Cleveland, OH

Handel Cherry Blossom - 16" Diam.
Kimball Sterling
Jonesboro, TN

Handel Floor Lamp with Harp Base
Kimball Sterling
Jonesboro, TN

Handel Mermaid Base
KImball Sterling
Jonesboro, TN

Handel Lamp
Kimball Sterling
Jonesboro, TN

Handel - 14" Diam.
Kimball Sterling
Jonesboro, TN

Handel Flower Lamp
Kimball Sterling
Jonesboro, TN

Handel Rose Vine - 16" Diam.
David Kurtz
Urbana, IL

Signed Handel Base & Shade - 18" Diam.
Private Collector

Handel Scenic - 18" Diam.
Private Collector

Handel "Harbor Scene" - 16" Diam.
Private Collector

Handel #6874 - 18" Diam.
Private Collector

Handel Scenic (Sponge Painted) - 18" Diam.
David Kurtz
Urbana, IL

Handel Lamp - 18" Diam.
Private Collector

Handel Panel Lamp
Hawaiian Overlay Scene - 20" Diam.
Private Collector

Handel Shade - 18" Diam.
Private Collector

Handel Shade "Mt. Fuji Scene" - 18" Diam.
Private Collector

Handel Scenic - 18" Diam.
Private Collector

Handel Panel Lamp
David Kurtz
Urbana, IL

Handel #190
Private Collector

Handel Elephantine Island Scene - 18" Diam.
Private Collector

Handel - 6 Paneled Lamp - 18" Diam.
Private Collector

Handel Conical Shaped
Scenic Landscape - 18" Diam.
Private Collector

Attributed To Handel
Private Collector

Handel Reverse Painted - 24" T, 18" Diam. Shade
Don Treadway Gallery
Cincinnati, OH

Handel Reverse Painted Landscape
Don Treadway Gallery
Cincinnati, OH

Handel Painted & Enameled Lamp
24" T, 18" Diam.
Don Treadway Gallery
Cincinnati, OH

Signed Handel #7555 - 25" T, 18" Diam.
Don Treadway Gallery
Cincinnati, OH

Handel with Leaf & Vine Design - 24" T, 18" Diam.
Don Treadway Gallery
Cincinnati, OH

Handel Bronze Harp Lamp with Gold Quezal Shade
Don Treadway Gallery
Cincinnati, OH

Handel Reverse Painted with Woodland Scene
#5854 - 24" T, 18" Diam. Shade
Don Treadway Gallery
Cincinnati, OH

Handel Shade on Rookwood Pottery Base
Marked Handel #6516 and #41 - 18" Diam.
Don Treadway Gallery
Cincinnati, OH

Handel Boudoir Lamp, Reverse Painted Landscape
Signed Handel #6451, 7" Diam. Shade, Base 15" T
Don Treadway Gallery
Cincinnati, OH

Handel Lamp - Shade Signed Handel #7281
24" T, 18" Diam.
Don Treadway Gallery
Cincinnati, OH

Handel Reverse Painted - Shade Signed & Numbered 6958 - 23" T, 16" Diam. Shade
Don Treadway Gallery
Cincinnati, OH

Handel Reverse Painted Boudoir Lamp
Shade Signed & Numbered #6905 - 13" T, 7" Diam.
Don Treadway Gallery
Cincinnati, OH

Handel Boudoir Lamp with Treasure
Island Shade, Signed #7165 - 7" Diam., 14" T
Don Treadway Gallery
Cincinnati, OH

Handel Desk Lamp - Bronzed Base
Shade 8" W x 12" T
Don Treadway Gallery
Cincinnati, OH

Handel Painted Lamp - Shade Signed
Handel #6547 - 18" Diam, 27" T
Don Treadway Gallery
Cincinnati, OH

Handel Boudoir Lamp - Reverse Painted
Mountain with Goldenrod & Foliage of
Yellow,Green and Brown, Bronze Base
Shade & Base Signed - 8" Diam. Shade, 14" T
Don Treadway Gallery
Cincinnati, OH

Handel Reverse Painted Landscape, Natural Colors
Shade Signed Handel #6643 - 18" Diam.
Don Treadway Gallery
Cincinnati, OH

Handel Shade on Teco Lamp
Shade is Mottled Green, Yellow & White
Shade Marked Handel - 19" Diam.
Don Treadway Gallery
Cincinnati, OH

Handel Leaded Glass Shade - Bronze Base Signed
Shade is Frosted Glass with Orange Circles
24" T, Shade 20 "Diam.
Don Treadway Gallery
Cincinnati, OH

Handel Lamp - Painted Shade - Marked
Red Flowers with Green Leaves on Brown Branches,
Yellow Background, Border of Red & Blue
Bronze Base, 24" T, 18" Diam. Shade
Don Treadway Gallery
Cincinnati, OH

Handel Reverse Painted Landscape, Natural Colors
Shade & Base Signed - 24" T, 18" Diam. Shade
Don Treadway Gallery
Cincinnati, OH

Handel Painted Lamp - Shade Signed #6431D
Green Shade, Bronzed Metal Base
24" T, 18" Diam. Shade
Don Treadway Gallery
Cincinnati, OH

Handel Lamp with Floral Overlay, Yellow and White
Slag Glass with Red Roses & Green Leaves
Shade & Base Signed - 24" T, 18" Diam.
Don Treadway Gallery
Cincinnati, OH

Handel Lamp - Shade & Base are Signed
23" T, 14" Diam. Brown Shade
Don Treadway Gallery
Cincinnati, OH

Handel Paneled Lamp with Bronze Overlay Scene
Shade is Green & Pink, Bronze Base
22" T, 14" Diam.
Don Treadway Gallery
Cincinnati, OH

1921 Handel Catalog Picture

1921 Handel Catalog Picture

1920 Handel Catalog Picture

1920 Handel Catalog Picture

1920's Handel Catalog Picture

Handel Leaded Lamp - 18" Diam.
Chris Olah - Century Antiques
Cleveland, OH

Signed Handel Boudoir Lamp - 7" Diam.
Chris Olah - Century Antiques
Cleveland, OH

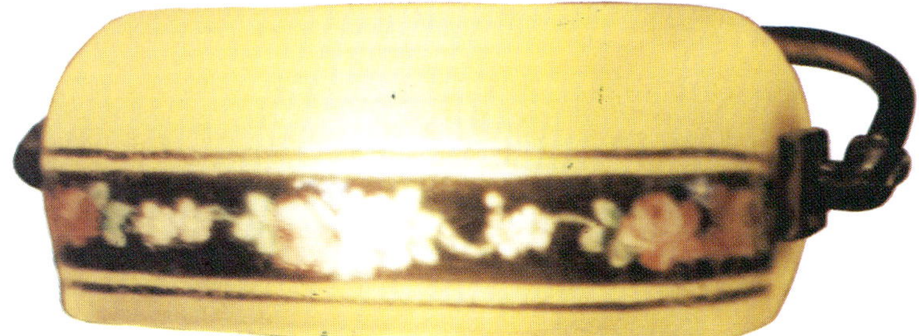

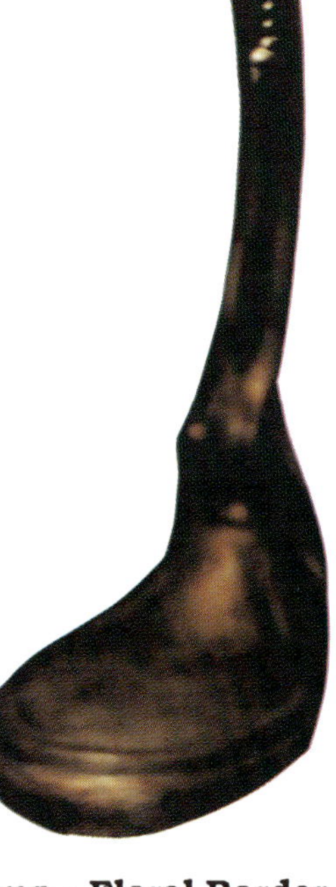

Signed Handel Desk Lamp - Floral Border
Chris Olah - Century Antiques
Cleveland, OH

Signed Handel Acid Cut Lamp - 18" Diam.
Chris Olah - Century Antiques
Cleveland, OH

Signed Handel "Chinese Pheasants" - 18" Diam.
Chris Olah - Century Antiques
Cleveland, OH

Signed Handel Scenic Desk Lamp (Large Size)
Chris Olah - Century Antiques
Cleveland, OH

Signed Handel Tropical Island Sunset Filigree Overlay - 16" Diam. Chris Olah - Century Antiques Cleveland, OH

Signed Handel Reverse Painted Lamp - 18" Diam. Chris Olah - Century Antiques Cleveland, OH

Signed Handel with Maple Leaf Border
Filigree Overlay - 18" Diam.
Chris Olah - Century Antiques
Cleveland, OH

Handel Reverse & Obverse Painted Lamp-14" Diam.
Chris Olah - Century Antiques
Cleveland, OH

Handel Leaded with Floral Border - 18" Diam.
Chris Olah - Century Antiques
Cleveland, OH

Signed Handel Reverse Painted Lamp - 18" Diam.
Chris Olah - Century Antiques
Cleveland, OH

Jeannette Lamps—Hand Decorated and Colors Fired In. 16-inch shades; height 22 inches. Note that these lamps have patented ring tops. All bases have felt covered bottom. Equipment and packing same as Group No. 500.
GROUP
800
No. 8-805
Finish—Italian Bronze
No. 8-624
Finish—Colonial Brass
No. 8-802
Finish—Antique Gold
No. 8-804
Finish—Black and Gold
No. 8-806
Finish—Venetian
No. 8-627
Finish—Antique Copper

No. 5-503
Finish—Chaldean
No. 5-368
Finish—Black and Gold
No. 5-513
Finish—Green Go
No. 5-516
Finish—Gold and Black
No. 5-508
Finish—Egyptian
No. 5-512
Finish—Arabian
Jeannette Lamps—Hand
GI
16-inch shades; height 22 inches.
lier pull sockets, six feet of silk cord
packed in a heavy shipping carton
shipping carton, assorted as shown.
insures you against breakage of sha
Julius And
M

No. 5-502
ish—Roman Gold
No. 5-515
Finish—Roman Gold
rated and Colors Fired In
500
s illustrated are equipped with Levo-
piece plugs. Each shade is carefully
reakage. Stands are packed six in a
s equipped with patented top which
ses have felt covered bottom.
& Sons Co.
ee
No. 5-504
Finish—Chaldean
No. 5-514
Finish—Roman Gold
No. 5-522
Finish—Chaldean
No. 5-507
Finish—Arabian

Jeannette Lamps—Hand Decorated and Colors Fired In. 12-inch shades; height 18 inches. Stands are equipped with one push through socket, six feet of silk cord and separable plug. All bases have felt covered bottom. Packed six lamps to a standard package.
GROUP
297
No. 7-512
Finish—Roman Gold
No. 7-515
Finish—Venetian Bronze
No. 7-514
Finish—Gold and Polychrome
No. 7-504
Finish—Bronze
No. 7-518
Finish—Bronze Green
No. 7-507
Finish—Silver and Polychrome

Signed Jefferson Lamp
Prater's Auction
East Palestine, OH

Signed Jefferson Lamp
Prater's Auction
East Palestine, OH

Jefferson Scenic Lamp
Prater's Auction
East Palestine, OH

Jefferson Shade on Glass Base - 18" Diam.
Artist Initialed "IN.B."
David Kurtz
Urbana, IL

Jefferson Scenic Lamp - 18" Diam.
David Kurtz
Urbana, IL

Jefferson Scenic Lamp - 18" Diam.
David Kurtz
Urbana, IL

Jefferson Scenic Lamp - 16" Diam.
David Kurtz
Urbana, IL

Signed Jefferson Reverse Painted Lamp - 18" Diam.
Chris Olah - Century Antiques
Cleveland, OH

Signed Jefferson Reverse Painted Lamp - 18" Diam.
Chris Olah - Century Antiques
Cleveland, OH

Miller Lamp with Overlay Design
Prater's Auction
East Palestine, OH

Miller Lamp with Scenic Overlay Design
Prater's Auction
East Palestine, OH

Miller Lamp with Scenic Overlay Design
Prater's Auction
East Palestine, OH

Miller Swan Scene with Overlay Design
Lites Top & Bottom - 18" Diam.
Prater's Auction
East Palestine, OH

Miller Lamp with Overlay Design
Kimball Sterling
Jonesboro, TN

Miller Lamp with Overlay Design
Kimball Sterling
Jonesboro, TN

Miller Lamp with Overlay Design
Kimball Sterling
Jonesboro, TN

Miller Lamp with Overlay Design
Kimball Sterling
Jonesboro, TN

Miller Leaded "Water Lillies & Cattails" - 18" Diam.
Chris Olah - Century Antiques
Cleveland, OH

Miller Leaded Lamp - 16" Diam.
Chris Olah - Century Antiques
Cleveland, OH

Moe Bridges Reverse Painted Lamp - 14 3/4" T
Prater's Auction
East Palestine, OH

Moe Bridges "Greek Ruins" - 18" Diam.
David Kurtz
Urbana, IL

Moe Bridges Chrysanthemum Floral - 18" Diam.
Private Collector

Moe Bridges Scenic #193 - 18" Diam.
Private Collector

1920's Pairpoint Reverse Painted Lamp
Shade & Base are Signed - 18' Diam.
McAllister Auction Service
Portland, MI

Pairpoint Lamp "Copley Shade"
Shade & Base are Signed
Prater's Auction
East Palestine, OH

Pairpoint Lamp - Shade & Base are Signed
Prater's Auction
East Palestine, OH

Pairpoint Scenic Lamp "Carlisle Shade"
Prater's Auction
East Palestine, OH

Pairpoint Puffy Boudoir Lamp
Floral Border & Lattice Decoration - 8" Diam.
Prater's Auction
East Palestine, OH

Pairpoint Scenic Landscape "Berkley Shade"
Prater's Auction
East Palestine, OH

Pairpoint Puffy Butterfly & Flowers
Prater's Auction
East Palestine, OH

Pairpoint Lamp - Shade & Base are Signed
Prater's Auction
East Palestine, OH

Pairpoint Scenic "Two Peacocks on Garden Wall"
Shade & Base are Signed - 16" Diam.
Prater's Auction
East Palestine, OH

Pairpoint "Birds of Paradise" Shade Signed - 18" Diam. Prater's Auction East Palestine, OH

Pairpoint Lamp "Exeter Shade" - 20" Diam. Shade Prater's Auction East Palestine, OH

Pairpoint Owl Lamp Base - 24" T
Signed at the Neck
Prater's Auction
East Palestine, OH

Pairpoint Lamp "Berkley Shade" - 20" Diam. Shade
Prater's Auction
East Palestine, OH

Pairpoint - 18" Diam. "Carlisle Shade"
Prater's Auction
East Palestine, OH

Pairpoint Lamp "New Bedford Harbor Scene"
Shade & Base are Signed - 20" Diam.
Prater's Auction
East Palestine, OH

Pairpoint "Exotic Bird" Exeter Shade
Kimball Sterling
Jonesboro, TN

Pairpoint Lamp "Butterfly & Roses"
Kimball Sterling
Jonesboro, TN

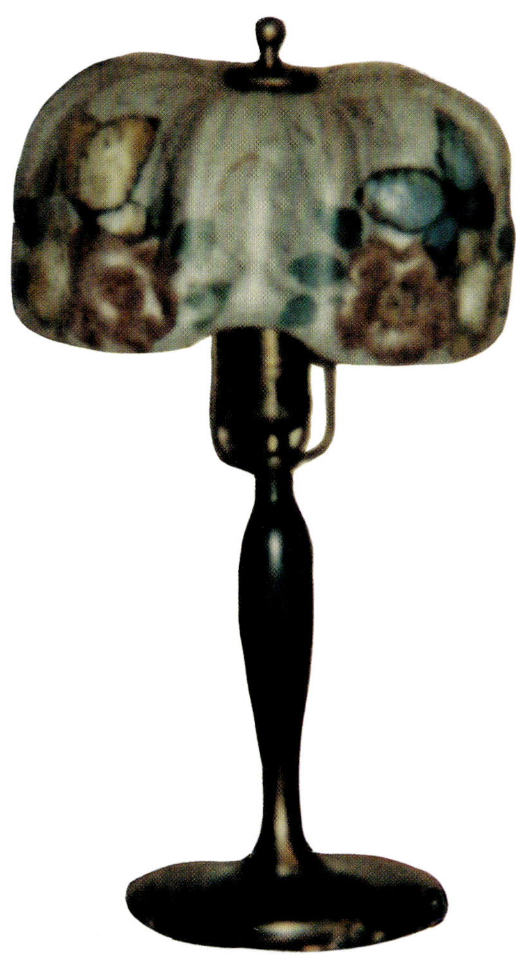

Pairpoint Lamp "Butterflies and Flowers"
Kimball Sterling
Jonesboro, TN

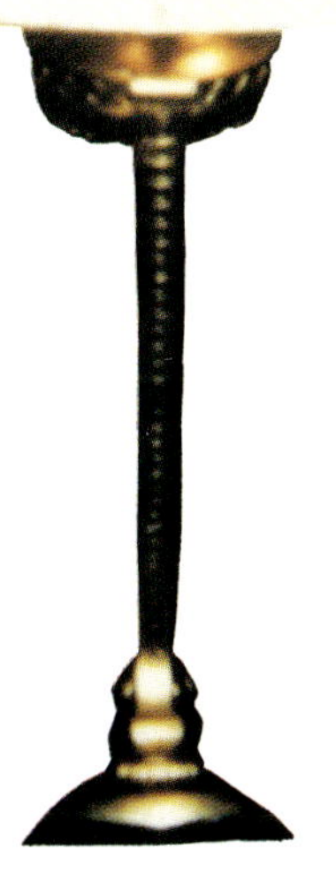

**Pairpoint "Copley Shade" - 18" Diam.
Prater's Auction
East Palestine, OH**

**Pairpoint Border Lamp "Berkley Shade"
Kimball Sterling
Jonesboro, TN**

Pairpoint Scenic Landscapen "Exeter Shade"
Kimball Sterling
Jonesboro, TN

Pairpoint Reverse Painted Lamp
Kimball Sterling
Jonesboro, TN

Pairpoint "Italian Garden" Scenic "Berkley Shade"
Kimball Sterling
Jonesboro, TN

Pairpoint Reverse Painted "Windmill"
Kimball Sterling
Jonesboro, TN

Pairpoint Lamp - 16" Diam.
Peach Lacy Design on Lucca Shade
Kimball Sterling
Jonesboro, TN

Pairpoint Puffy Tulip
Kimball Sterling
Jonesboro, TN

Pairpoint "Italian Garden Scene"
"Berkley Shade" - 20" Diam.
Private Collector

Signed Pairpoint "Carlisle Shade"- 18" Diam.
David Kurtz
Urbana, IL

Pairpoint "Forest Scene with Deer"
"Berkley Shade" - 18" Diam.
Private Collector

Pairpont "Garden of Allah" Scenic
"Carlisle Shade" - 18" Diam.
David Kurtz
Urbana, IL

Pairpoint #202 "Carlisle Shade"
David Kurtz
Urbana, IL

Pairpoint "Butterflies" - 15" Diam.
Private Collector

Pairpoint "English Country Scene"
"Carlisle Shade" - 18" Diam.
David Kurtz
Urbana, IL

Pairpoint Lamp "Exeter Shade" - 16 1/2" Diam.
David Kurtz
Urbana, IL

Pairpoint Scenic Lamp
"Lansdowne Shade" - 20" Diam.
Private Collector

Pairpoint "Venetian Harbor Scene on Dolphin Base"
"Lansdowne Shade"
Private Collector

Pairpoint Boudoir Lamp - Puffy Flowers
14" T, 18" Diam. Shade
Don Treadway Gallery
Cincinnati, OH

Pairpoint Art Deco Lamp
23" T, 14" Diam. Shade
Don Treadway Gallery
Cincinnati, OH

Pairpoint Puffy Lamp, Molded Blown-out Reverse Painted "Poppy" Shade
Base is Signed - 23" T, 14" Diam. Shade
Don Treadway Gallery
Cincinnati, OH

Pairpoint Scenic Lamp - 15 1/2" Diam.
Artist Signed "Durand"
Chris Olah - Century Antiques
Cleveland, OH

Signed Pairpoint Lamp "Berkley Shade" - 18" Diam.
Chris Olah - Century Antiques
Cleveland, OH

Pairpoint Scenic Lamp - 18" Diam.
Artist Signed "F. Raye"
Chris Olah - Century Antiques
Cleveland, OH

Signed Pairpoint Scenic Lamp
"Chesterfield Shade" - 14" Diam.
Chris Olah - Century Antiques
Cleveland, OH

Signed Pairpoint Reversed Painted Lamp-16" Diam.
Chris Olah - Century Antiques
Cleveland, OH

Signed Pairpoint Reverse Painted Lamp
"Copley Shade" Artist Signed "Durand" - 18" Diam.
Chris Olah - Century Antiques
Cleveland, OH

Signed Pairpoint Reverse Painted Lamp
"Carlisle Shade" - 20" Diam.
Chris Olah - Century Antiques
Cleveland, OH

Signed Pairpoint Reverse Painted
"Berkley Shade" - 18" Diam.
Chris Olah - Century Antiques
Cleveland, OH

Signed Pairpoint Puffy Lamp - 20" T, 14" Diam.
James Roush - Antiques Ltd.
Marion, IN

Pairpoint "Garden of Allah" Scenic Lamp
Base & Shade are Signed - 16" Diam.
James Roush - Antiques Ltd.
Marion, IN

Pairpoint Scenic Lamp on Dolphin Base
Base & Shade are Signed - 14" Diam.
James Roush - Antiques Ltd.
Marion, IN

Signed Pairpoint "Red Poppy"
Edward Malakoff - Pairpoint Lamp Museum
River Edge, NJ

Signed Pairpoint Stratford Hummingbird
Edward Malakoff - Pairpoint Lamp Museum
River Edge, NJ

Signed Pairpoint Rose Bouquet
Edward Malakoff - Pairpoint Lamp Museum
River Edge, NJ

Signed Pairpoint, Berkeley Shade
"Treasure Island" Scenic
Edward Malakoff - Pairpoint Lamp Museum
River Edge, NJ

Signed Pairpoint, Livorna Shade
Edward Malakoff - Pairpoint Lamp Museum
River Edge, NJ

Signed Pairpoint "Lotus Puffy Shade"
Edward Malakoff - Pairpoint Lamp Museum
River Edge, NJ

Signed Pairpoint "Bombay Shade"
Scenic Landscape - 18" Diam.
Edward Malakoff - Pairpoint Lamp Museum
River Edge, NJ

Signed Pairpoint Floral
"Lansdowne Shade" - 16" Diam.
Edward Malakoff - Pairpoint Lamp Museum
River Edge, NJ

Signed Pairpoint "Berkeley Shade"
Dark Floral - 18" Diam.
Edward Malakoff - Pairpoint Lamp Museum
River Edge, NJ

Signed Pairpoint "Directorie Shade with Floral Border" - 18" Diam.
Edward Malakoff - Pairpoint Lamp Museum
River Edge, NJ

Phoenix Scenic Lamp
Prater's Auction
East Palestine, OH

Phoenix Lamp
Prater's Auction
East Palestine, OH

Phoenix Scenic Lamp
Prater's Auction
East Palestine, OH

Phoenix Scenic Lamp - 18" Diam.
Prater's Auction
East Palestine, OH

Phoenix Scenic Lamp - 23" T, 16" Diam.
Prater's Auction
East Palestine, OH

Phoenix Scenic Lamp - 16" Diam.
David Kurtz
Urbana, IL

Phoenix Scenic Lamp - 18" Diam.
David Kurtz
Urbana, IL

Phoenix Scenic Lamp - 18" Diam.
Private Collector

Phoenix Scenic Lamp - 18" Diam.
David Kurtz
Urbana, IL

Phoenix Scenic Lamp - 18" Diam.
David Kurtz
Urbana, IL

Phoenix Scenic Lamp - 16" Diam.
David Kurtz
Urbana, IL

Phoenix Scenic Lamp - 18" Diam.
David Kurtz
Urbana, IL

Phoenix Scenic Lamp - 18" Diam.
David Kurtz
Urbana, IL

Phoenix "Taj-Ma-Hal" Scenic Lamp - 18" Diam.
David Kurtz
Urbana, IL

Believed to be Phoenix Shade - 16" Diam.
David Kurtz
Urbana, IL

Phoenix Reverse Painted Scenic Lamp - 18" Diam.
Chris Olah - Century Antiques
Cleveland, OH

Phoenix Reverse Painted Lamp - 18" Diam.
Chris Olah - Century Antiques
Cleveland, OH

Phoenix Reverse Painted Lamp - 16" Diam.
Chris Olah - Century Antiques
Cleveland, OH

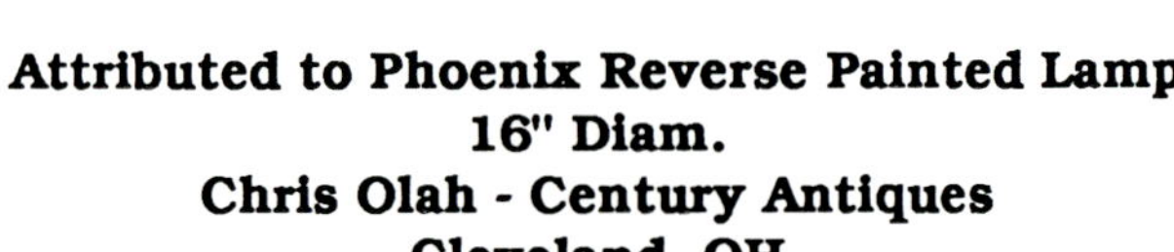

Attributed to Phoenix Reverse Painted Lamp
16" Diam.
Chris Olah - Century Antiques
Cleveland, OH

Pittsburgh Scenic Lamp
Prater's Auction
East Palestine, OH

Pittsburgh Scenic Lamp
Prater's Auction
East Palestine, OH

Pittsburgh Reverse Painted Lamp
Kimball Sterling
Jonesboro, TN

Pittsburgh Lamp - 14" Diam.
Private Collector

Pittsburgh Scenic Lamp
Kimball Sterling
Jonesboro, TN

Pittsburgh Dome Shade
"Call of the Wild" - 18" Diam.
David Kurtz
Urbana, IL

Pittsburgh Water Scene - 16" Diam.
David Kurtz
Urbana, IL

Pittsburgh - 16" Diam. Shade
David Kurtz
Urbana, IL

Pittsburgh "Autumn Leaves" - 18" Diam.
David Kurtz
Urbana, IL

Pittsburgh Obverse & Reverse Painted Scenic Lamp - 18" Diam.
David Kurtz
Urbana, IL

Pittsburgh Reverse Painted Panel Lamp
Private Collector

Signed Pittsburgh Scenic Lamp
"9 Lakes of Killarney" - 16" Diam.
David Kurtz
Urbana, IL

Pittsburgh Boudoir Scenic Lamp
David Kurtz
Urbana, IL

Pittsburgh Lamp - Beehive Shade - 18" Diam.
David Kurtz
Urbana, IL

Pittsburgh Winter Scene - 16" Diam.
David Kurtz
Urbana, IL

Pittsburgh Sheep Scene - 14" Diam.
David Kurtz
Urbana, IL

Pittsburgh Obverse & Reverse Painted
Scenic Lamp - 16" Diam.
Chris Olah - Century Antiques
Cleveland, OH

Pittsburgh Reverse Painted Lamp - 16" Diam.
Chipped Ice Finish
Chris Olah - Century Antiques
Cleveland, OH

Pittsburgh Obverse & Reverse Painted Lamp
Rocky Mountain Scene
Chris Olah - Century Antiques
Cleveland, OH

Rookwood Lamp, Originally an Oil Burner
#1078
Cincinnati Art Gallery
Cincinnati, OH

Rookwood Lamp, 1948, #2785, 13" T
Cincinnati Art Gallery
Cincinnati, OH

Rookwood Lamp, This is a Factory Made Lamp, 1903, #51 AZ
Height of Pottery is 10" - Shade is not original.
Cincinnati Art Gallery
Cincinnati, OH

Rookwood Pottery Lamp Base - 19 3/4" T
Artist Signed "John Dee Wareham", #426Z
Cincinnati Art Gallery
Cincinnati, OH

Rookwood Pottery Lamp Base, #925B
Base Is Marked with Rookwood Logo - 13 1/4" T
Cincinnati Art Gallery
Cincinnati, OH

Roycroft Lamp
Private Collector

Roycroft Hammered Copper Lamp - 20" T
Don Treadway Gallery
Cincinnati, OH

Roycroft Lamp #903 - 14" T
Dark Reddish Brown & Mica Shade
Don Treadway Gallery
Cincinnati, OH

Roycroft Hammered Copper Desk Lamp #906, 13" T
Don Treadway Gallery
Cincinnati, OH

Tiffany Lamp Signed Tiffany & Co.
Prater's Auction
East Palestine, OH

Signed Tiffany Shade & Base
Prater's Auction
East Palestine, OH

Tiffany Lamp Signed Tiffany Studios N.Y.
22" T, 17 1/2" Diam. Shade
Prater's Auction
East Palestine, OH

Tiffany Desk Lamp, Bronze Base With Verdigris
Finish - 14" T, Base Marked Tiffany Studios N.Y.
Garth's Auction Inc.
Delaware, OH

L.C. Tiffany Lamp, Originally an Oil Burner
"Autumn Leaf" - 16" Diam.
Kimball Sterling
Jonesboro, TN

Tiffany Acorn Lamp, Originally an Oil Burner
Kimball Sterling
Jonesboro, TN

Tiffany Lamp "Dogwood"
Kimball Sterling
Jonesboro, TN

L.C. Tiffany "Turtleback" Lamp
Kimball Sterling
Jonesboro, TN

Tiffany Linen Fold Glass & Bronze Table Lamp
Shade & Base are Marked - 22" T, 14" Diam.
Don Treadway Gallery
Cincinnati, OH

Tiffany Studios Telescoping Table Lamp #28596
26" T, Shade Signed L.C.T.
Don Treadway Gallery
Cincinnati, OH

L.C. Tiffany Three Light Lily Lamp #9521
Base Signed Tiffany Studios N.Y. & Numbered,
Shades Signed L.C.T.
Don Treadway Gallery
Cincinnati, OH

Tiffany Desk Lamp, Base of Bronze Clad Pottery
Marked with L.C.T. & Tiffany Bronze Pottery- 15" T
Shade Signed "L.C.T. Favrile" - 7"Diam.
Don Treadway Gallery
Cincinnati, OH

Tiffany Counter Balance Desk Lamp, Shade Signed "L.C. Tiffany Favrile" - 7" Diam., Base Signed "Tiffany Studios, N.Y. #417" - 18" T
Don Treadway Gallery
Cincinnati, OH

Tiffany Turtleback Glass & Bronze Lamp, Base is Signed "Tiffany Studios, New York #541" - 14" T
Don Treadway Gallery
Cincinnati, OH

Tiffany Ten Lily Glass & Bronze Table Lamp, Shades Signed "L.C.T.", Base Signed "Tiffany Studios, N.Y. #381" - 22" T
Don Treadway Gallery
Cincinnati, OH

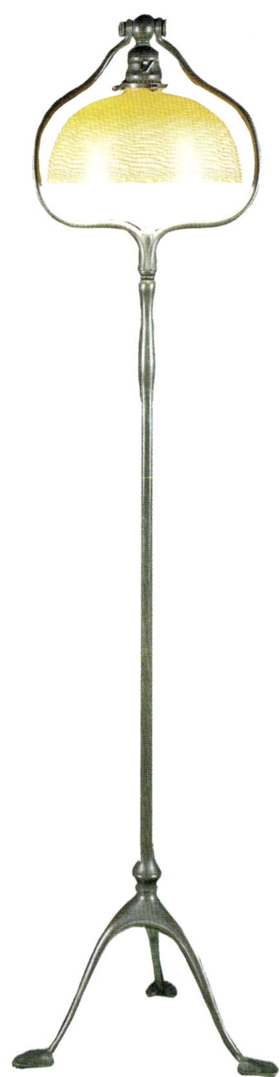

Tiffany Bronze & Glass Floor Lamp, Base Signed "Tiffany Studios, N.Y. #423" - 55" T, Shade Signed "L.C.T. Favrile" - 10" Diam.
Don Treadway Gallery
Cincinnati, OH

Tiffany Geometric Leaded Shade on Bronze Stick Base #618, Metal Tag in Shade "Tiffany Studios" & Base Impressed Same - 17 1/2" T
Don Treadway Gallery
Cincinnati, OH

Tiffany #424 Lamp Base with Gold Steuben Shade 17 1/2" T, Both are Signed
Don Treadway Gallery
Cincinnati, OH

Tiffany Lamp "Acorn" Leaded Glass, Bronze Base #181, Shade & Base Are Signed - 20" T, 16" Diam.
Don Treadway Gallery
Cincinnati, OH

Tiffany Geometric Leaded Glass & Bronze Table Lamp, Shade Signed with Metal Tag "Tiffany Studio, N.Y. #1469" - 18" Diam., Base Signed "Tiffany Studios, N.Y. #587" - 22" T
Don Treadway Gallery
Cincinnati, OH

Tiffany Shade on Grueby Base - 16" Diam. Shade
Don Treadway Gallery
Cincinnati, OH

Tiffany Leaded Glass & Bronze Base Lamp, Base
Signed & Numbered #21219 - 19" T, 12" Diam.
Various Shades of Green & White & Yellow Acorns
Don Treadway Gallery
Cincinnati, OH

Tiffany Leaded Glass Table Lamp, Base Signed
#533, Shade Signed #1913 - 22" T, 18" Diam.
Yellow & White Glass, Original Gold Dore' Patina
Don Treadway Gallery
Cincinnati, OH

Tiffany Lamp with Geometric Shade & Bronze Base,
Shade & Base Signed "Tiffany Studios, N.Y." Base
Impressed #531 - 26" T, 20" Diam., Green Glass
Don Treadway Gallery
Cincinnati, OH

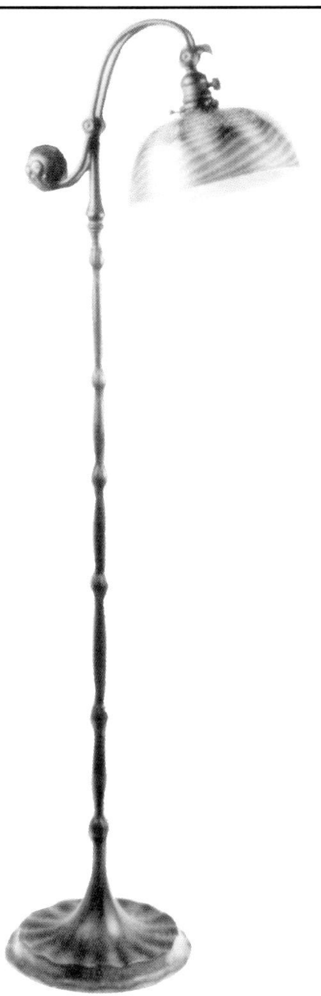

Tiffany Lamp, Base Signed "L.C. Tiffany Studios, N.Y. #677",Shade Signed "L.C.T. Favrile"- 10" Diam. Shade is Green & Yellow, Bronze Base Don Treadway Gallery Cincinnati, OH

Tiffany Bellflower Lamp, Base Impressed "Tiffany Studios #6841" - 22" T, Shade Signed "Tiffany Studios, N.Y." - 16" Diam., Shade has Deep Red & Pink Bellflowers among Yellow & Green Foliage Don Treadway Gallery Cincinnati, OH

(Left & Right) Tiffany Studios Candlesticks, Signed "Tiffany Studios, N.Y. #650 Gold Dore' Finish- 15" T
(Middle) Tiffany Studios Three Lily Glass & Bronze Lamp, Gold Favrile Shades Signed "L.C.T.",
Base Signed "Tiffany Studios, N.Y. #310" - 13" T
Don Treadway Gallery
Cincinnati, OH

Tiffany Bronze & Glass Ceiling Fixture, Shade Signed "L.C.T" - 7" x 16"
Golden Yellow Turtlebacks with Brown Glass Globe
Don Treadway Gallery
Cincinnati, OH

Tiffany Lily Lamp, Marked "Tiffany Studios, N.Y. #305", Base #5981
Gold Shades & Bronze Base - 22" T
Don Treadway Gallery
Cincinnati, OH

Signed Wilkinson - 24" T, 16 1/2" Diam.
Prater's Auction
East Palestine, OH

Wilkinson Lamp
Kimball Sterling
Jonesboro, TN

Wilkinson Lamp
Kimball Sterling
Jonesboro, TN

Signed Wilkinson - 20" Diam.
David Kurtz
Urbana, IL

Wilkinson Lamp #182 - 20 1/2" Diam.
Private Collector

Wilkinson Lamp
Kimball Sterling
Jonesboro, TN

Elizabeth Eaton Burton Shell Lamp, Signed "eBe" within Oval - 21" T (Elizabeth Burton was a California Artist Who Worked in the Arts & Crafts Style.)
Brass Lily Pad Base, Glass Petal Shades
Don Treadway Gallery
Cincinnati, OH

Empire Panel Lamp
David Kurtz
Urbana, IL

Galle "Dragon Fly" Lamp
Private Collector

La Verre Francais Cameo Lamp - 13" T x 6" W
Don Treadway Gallery
Cincinnati, OH

Limbert Arts & Crafts Lamp, Hammered Copper Base, - 24" T, 26" Diam. Shade, 9" Diam. of Bottom of Base Don Treadway Gallery Cincinnati, OH

Mushroom Shade of Loetz Glass on Pairpoint Base 20" T x 12" Diam. Don Treadway Gallery Cincinnati, OH

Marblehead Decorated Pottery Lamp
Pottery - 8"x 8" T, Total Height 21"
9" Glass Globe (Extremely Rare Lamp, Believed to be the Only One to Ever Surface at Auction)
Don Traedway Gallery
Cincinnati, OH

Royal Art Glass Lamp
Kimball Sterling
Jonesboro, TN

Salem Brothers Lamp
Prater's Auction
East Palestine, OH

Steuben Side Mantle Lamps, Shades Signed
Prater's Auction
East Palestine, OH

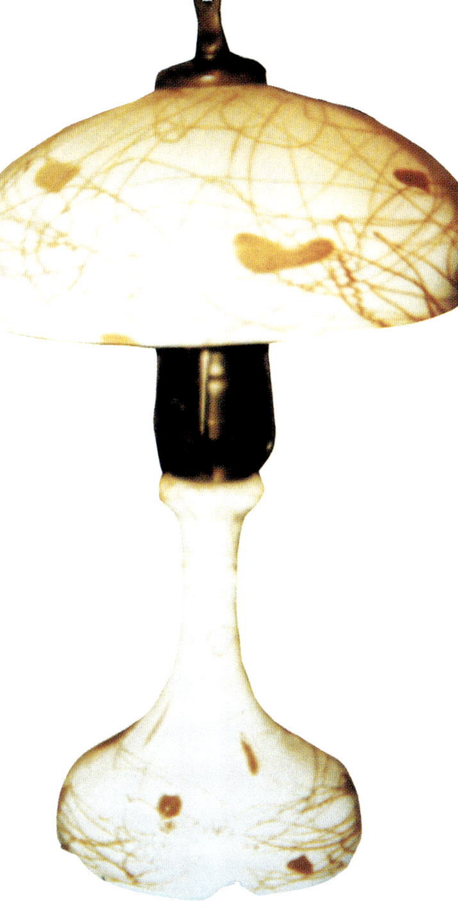

Steuben Lamp
Prater's Auction
East Palestine, OH

Williamson Leaded Glass Lamp, Metal Base
Green & Brown Glass Shade, 8" Diam. Shade, 25" T
Don Treadway Gallery
Cincinnati, OH

Williamson Lamp, Bronze Base with Swirled Bottom in Art Nouveau Style
25" T, 18" Diam.
Don Treadway Gallery
Cincinnati, OH

Signed Bradley & Hubbard
Leaded Lamp - 18" Diam.
Chris Olah - Century Antiques
Cleveland, OH

Signed Czechoslovakian Beaded Lamp
James Roush - Antiques Ltd.
Marion, IN

Duffner & Kimberly Leaded Lamp in Adams Style - 20" Diam.
Chris Olah - Century Antiques
Cleveland, OH

DKCo

The Louis XV lamp

The elegance and the delicate symmetry of this lamp represent charmingly the exquisite beauty of the reign of Louis XV. Suitable for Drawing room or Boudoir designed after this Period

Lighting fixtures of all kinds for the dining room, library, drawing room, hall and boudoir, harmonizing with the design of the room. These designs are most beautiful, and comprise a full line of fixtures, not to be obtained elsewhere.

Electric lamps representing all the periods from the classic to the modern are on exhibition and sale at our especially designed show rooms, eighth floor, 11 West 32nd Street, New York, or at the following:

Theodore B. Starr, New York City
Smith Patterson Company, Boston, Mass.
Dulin & Martin Company, Inc., Washington, D. C.
John S. Bradstreet & Company, Minneapolis, Minn.
F. A. Robbins Company, Springfield, Mass.
Morreau Gas Fixture Mfg. Co., Cleveland, Ohio
The Toledo Chandelier Mfg. Company, Toledo, O.
The Hofman Jewelry Company, Columbus, Ohio
The Fixture House Company, Kansas City, Mo.
Morgan & Allen Company, Sole Agents for the Pacific Coast

The Bailey, Banks & Biddle Co., Philadelphia, Pa.
W. K. Cowan & Company, Chicago, Ill.
Dauler, Close & Johns, Pittsburg, Pa.
Forve-Pettebone Company, Los Angeles, Cal.
Orchard & Wilhelm Carpet Company, Omaha, Neb.
Walbridge & Company, Buffalo, N. Y.
The Sanborn-Marsh Electric Co., Indianapolis, Ind.
Pioneer Mantel and Fixture Co., Detroit, Mich.
Tilden-Thurber Company, Providence, R. I.
Frank Adam Electric Company, St. Louis, Mo.

Dept. F.

THE DUFFNER AND KIMBERLY COMPANY
11 WEST 32D STREET NEW YORK

1907 Magazine Ad

Signed Fulper Pottery Lamp - 18" Diam.
James Roush - Antiques Ltd.
Marion, IN

Galle' Leaf Designed Bronze Base
Called a Corolla - 20" T
James Roush - Antiques Ltd.
Marion, IN

Signed Handel Paneled Lamp with Peacock Feathers Design - 24" T
James Roush - Antiques Ltd.
Marion, IN

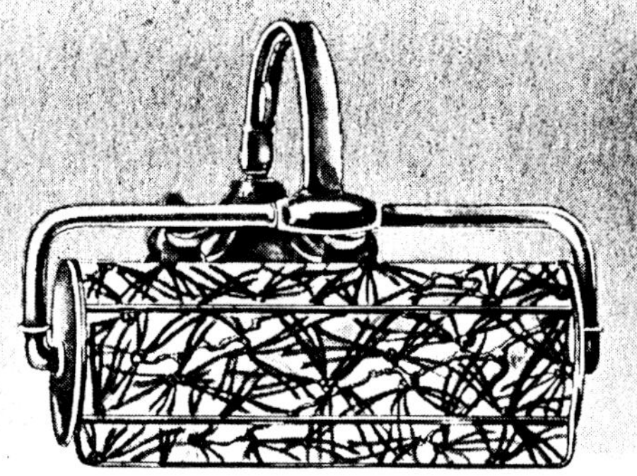

Are You Satisfied With Your Home Lighting?

Handel Lamps and Lighting Fixtures furnish splendid illumination for every purpose. They are artistically perfect in every detail.

Handel Lamps

For Desk or Boudoir

The lamps pictured here are typical of the many artistic desk or boudoir lamps bearing the Handel name. Their dainty size (about fifteen inches high), their delicate coloring and graceful construction render them admirably suited for the boudoir or desk.

They make very acceptable Christmas gifts. Put them on your list now.

The Handel productions comprise many styles of lamps and lighting fixtures for electricity gas or oil. They are sold by leading jewelers and lighting fixture dealers. Look for the name "Handel" on every lamp.

Write for our booklet "Suggestions for Good Lighting"

THE HANDEL CO.

382 East Main Street Meriden, Conn.

New York Showrooms: 64 Murray Street

1911 Magazine Ad

» » VARIED LAMPS *by* HANDEL *for* OLD *and* NEW ROOMS » »

The lamp below is a modernistic and yet conservative design suitable for use with most types of furniture groupings. The base is of bright pewter in combination with black ebony, while the shade is hand-painted silver and black on skintex. Height 20" over all.

This Handel lamp was especially designed for use with furnishings of that period of our history usually referred to as the Federal era. The lamp, of exquisite workmanship, is styled with a hand-painted shade, covered and lined with honeydew silk. The base is finished in weathered old brass with eagles in Colonial gilt. Size 22½" over all.

The Handel bridge lamp above correctly interprets the Empire period. The base is beautifully finished in empire green and antique gilt. It is 61" high and has an arm which raises and lowers and adjusts to any position. The shade is hand-painted under light gold pleated silk and lined with honeydew silk.

THE effectiveness of any given example of interior decoration is based primarily upon what it achieves in point of "suitability". This element of suitability has been taken into account in all Handel Lamp designs; some carry the fine things that tradition has brought them and yet strike a new note, while others are unrelated to tradition and are smartly new. All are keyed to our time and express our present feeling for elegance with restraint.

We cordially invite the architect, the decorator, and the home-owner to visit our showrooms or if that is not convenient, to write us a description of the type of lamp desired.

THE HANDEL COMPANY

MAKERS OF

HANDEL LAMPS & LIGHTING FIXTURES

200 Fifth Ave., New York • Meriden, Connecticut

1930 Magazine Ad

16-inch, 2-light lamp, antique gold finish, amber glass shade.

MILLER

Portable Lamps

MILLER Lamps combine artistic design, sound construction and moderate price. They make their appeal to those who appreciate utility when expressed in terms of beauty.

The Library Lamp here illustrated has a purity of line and a refinement of detail which makes it suitable for any living room which is furnished in good taste.

The price is very moderate, which is made possible by the coöperative buying of the companies below listed. They will be glad to show you this lamp or to answer inquiries by mail.

For Sale by

Brooklyn Edison Co., Brooklyn, N. Y.
Chattanooga Railway & Light Co., Chattanooga, Tenn.
Commonwealth Edison Co., Chicago, Ill.
Consolidated Gas, Electric Light and Power Co., Baltimore, Md.
Dallas Power and Light Co., Dallas, Texas
Subsidiaries of Henry L. Doherty & Co., In various cities
Eastern Shore Gas & Electric Co., In various cities
Edison Electric Illuminating Co. of Boston, Boston, Mass.
The Electric Shop, Providence, R. I.
The Hartford Electric Light Co., Hartford, Conn.
Indianapolis Light & Heat Co., Indianapolis, Ind.
Kansas City Light and Power Co., Kansas City, Mo.
Kansas Gas and Electric Co., Wichita, Kan.
Little Rock Railway & Electric Co., Little Rock, Ark.
Minneapolis General Electric Co., Minneapolis, Ind.
Nashville Railway & Light Co., Nashville, Tenn.
Nebraska Power Co., Omaha, Neb.
Penn. Central Light & Power Co., In various cities
Philadelphia Electric Co., Philadelphia, Pa.
Portland Light & Power Co., Portland, Ore.
Potomac Electric Power Co., Washington, D. C.
Public Service Electric Co., In various cities in New Jersey
Public Service Co., In various cities in Northern Ill.
Sioux City Gas and Electric Co., Sioux City, Iowa
Utah Power and Light Co., Salt Lake City
Union Electric Light & Power Co., St. Louis, Mo.
United Electric Light and Power Co., New York City

And Electric Light Companies in other cities in the United States.

CANADIAN DISTRIBUTORS: Canadian General Electric Co., Ltd., Toronto, Ont.

Edward Miller & Company

Established 1844

Meriden Connecticut

1920 Magazine Ad

Signed Moe Bridges Scenic Lamp - 15" Diam.
Chris Olah - Century Antiques
Cleveland, OH

Moe Bridges Scenic Lamp - 18" Diam.
David Kurtz
Urbana, IL

Oscar Bach Leaded Lamp
Private Owner

Phoenix Reverse Painted Scenic Lamp - 18" Diam.
David Kurtz
Urbana, IL

Phoenix Reverse Painted Scenic Lamp - 14" Diam.
David Kurtz
Urbana, IL

Pittsburgh Scenic Lamp with Overlay Design
David Kurtz
Urbana, IL

Pittsburgh Scenic Lamp - 18" Diam.
Private Owner

Pittsburgh Lamp with Floral Design
Private Owner

Signed Pair of Stained Glass Lamps from Spain
Electric-Bronze Base
House of Antieks
Synder, TX

Signed Steuben with Peacocks Design on Base
Cloth Shade - 16" T
James Roush - Antiques Ltd.
Marion, IN

Carved Tiffany Glass Lamp
with Yellow Daffodils Design - 15" T
James Roush - Antiques Ltd.
Marion, IN

Wilkinson Leaded Lamp
Oriental Poppies Design - 20" Diam.
Chris Olah - Century Antiques
Cleveland, OH

Signed Western Lamp & Brassworks Leaded Lamp with Tree Base
Chris Olah - Century Antiques
Cleveland, OH